Self-Esteem

Concepts for Activities, Discussion and Insights

**Retold, adapted and written by
Greta Barclay Lipson, Ed.D.**

illustrated by Dan Grossmann

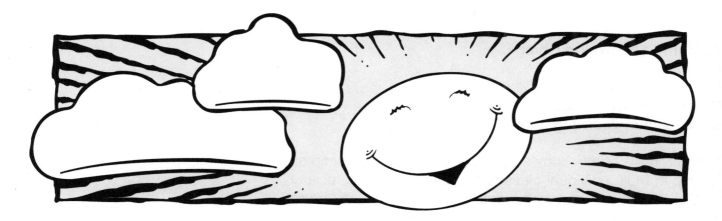

Teaching & Learning Company

A Lorenz company
P.O. Box 802
Dayton OH 45401-0802
www.teachinglearning.com

This book belongs to

_____

Cover by Dan Grossman

Copyright © 1997, Teaching & Learning company

ISBN No. 978-1-57310-080-9

Printing No. 987654321

Teaching & Learning Company
A Lorenz company
P.O. Box 802
Dayton, OH 45401-0802
www.teachinglearning.com

At the time of publication, every effort was made to ensure the accuracy of the information included in this book. However, we cannot guarantee that the agencies and organizations mentioned will continue to operate or to maintain these current locations.

TLC10080

Especially for Rachel, Joseph,
Alexander and Madeleine with
enduring love.

TLC10080

Table of Contents

Listen Up: A Poem from Teacher to Student

Tell Us Who You Are
(Professor Covensky)

You Are One of a Kind
(Clotho and Her Sisters)

Be Kind and You Will Receive Kindness
(Androcles and the Lion)

Choose Your Friends Wisely
(Cat and Mouse in Partnership)

Happiness Comes from Within
(The Shirt Off His Back)

TLC10080

People Are Beautiful Because We Love Them
(A Crack in the Wall)

You Are a fine Creation
(The Belly and Its Members)

Believe in Yourself
(Beowulf)

Care About Something Outside of Yourself
(With All My Heart)

What Really Counts Is What's Inside You
(TGTBT Building)

You Are Finer Than You Think
(Redhead)

Do not accuse nature. She has done her part. Now you do yours.

–John Milton

Dear Teacher or Parent,

The difficulty in writing a book on self-esteem is that everyone agrees that self-esteem in one's life is critical to development—but exactly how one manages to help a youngster build self-esteem is the great stumbling block. If you are not the child's parent, it is even more problematic, especially if the children involved don't think they are worth much to begin with and all of their experience confirms it.

We would hope, for all children, that they have loving parents, a good home life, caring relatives or extended family, economic security, a health and safe environment and a promising future. But for many children these conditions are an ideal that has nothing to do with their reality. It is popular to repeat the incantations, "I am somebody," "I am special," "I am a universe of wonder,"—but this doesn't make it so, nor does it convince a child with a fragile ego!

Since school has become a repository for society's pathology and there is so much that we are powerless to overcome, how (you may ask) do we dare presume that we can make a difference to the child who needs our affirmation? Based upon experience as a parent and educator I do believe, with all my heart, that teachers and concerned adults can sometimes make a difference in the face of discouraging odds. Teachers can make a difference because they have access to the psyche and innards of children. We share significant time together during which time we talk, work and play. Most importantly we are given the opportunity to acknowledge the efforts and good points of children in our care.

In the course of a term—a semester—or a few weeks, however brief or protracted the time spent together—it is possible to make a difference in the perception that children have of themselves. You may not make a significant contribution to every child's development, but as a teacher you must always try.

What is more, you must include all you students in supportive roles toward one another! Teach them civility and consideration toward themselves and others. You may never know about your significant imprint on a child's soul or future—and therein lies a kind of spiritual magic. The awareness that you can shape a young life gives teaching its loftiest goal.

Be kind to your students. Set an example of respect, cooperation and regard for each other individual. Listen to one another. Support every effort. Discourage demeaning behavior. Create an atmosphere of psychological safety for the children in your class. Endeavor to say something complimentary and heartening to each student—however hard that stretch may be. We are not suggesting excess nor do we encourage effusive compliments at every turn. But protect and nurture those tender young shoots. Above all—be a model of humanity.

I believe earnestly in this approach because such teachers were a strong influence in my life. One teacher in particular put me on the right path when I was adrift because I had dropped out of school at a very young age. He changed my life because he had confidence in my ability (when I did not) and he told me so—quietly and earnestly, without fanfare. It took me 30 years to find him again so that I could say "Thank you."

This is a true-to-life book.

Sincerely,

Greta

Greta Barclay Lipson, Ed.D.

TLC10080

Set the Stage

For a Life-Affirming Learning Environment

The teacher is the model for kindness, tolerance, respect and civility!

Building Toward Self-Esteem

- Create a positive classroom environment. Build psychological safety where students can participate freely–an atmosphere where taking a chance on an answer, an idea or creative expression does not pose a personal risk.

- Help your students learn to validate each other at appropriate times, e.g. "That was a neat idea." "You're a super player." "I'm glad I'm on your team!"

- Develop a cooperative classroom where there is trust in working together toward common goals–as opposed to a competitive classroom with winners and losers.

- Strive for group cohesiveness and loyalty.

- Stress personal responsibility and harmonious interaction with others which generates good feelings.

- Demonstrate how to be kind and supportive by words and deeds in every working day together–where no one is ever demeaned.

- Explain that there is no one who can do everything well–nor does anyone have to do everything well.

- Discuss intelligence, skills and aptitudes in terms of a constellation of abilities–those combinations which are different in all of us in infinite array.

- Liken the exciting breadth and range of potential in each person to a kaleidoscope, both concrete and metaphorical. Bring a kaleidoscope to class to illustrate this manifold concept.

Set the Stage

A Message from the Teacher to the Students

Think of your classroom as a team, a caring community or a tribe. You are all here for the same purpose–to learn together, to help one another, to respect yourself and others. Try to be the best that you can be and remember: Nobody in this world knows everything (not even the teacher)!

Some lessons will be hard and some will be easy, but every one of us will make an effort. There will be good days and bad days. There is always a fresh new day to look forward to, and we will make it possible for each of us to have our day in the sun. We will promise to listen to everyone who has something to say–all in good time. We will never laugh or ridicule or make a person feel bad.

We will try our best to make others feel pleased to be a member of our group. Remember to treat others as you want to be treated and that attitude will make our classroom a good, happy place to learn.

Activities

Based upon the ideas listed above, discuss the golden rules of your classroom and the proj-ects which capture the cooperative spirit as listed above.

- Try to be the best person you can be and then be proud of yourself!

- Create a class banner or logo with the room number, and perhaps a sunburst, a bright star, a rainbow or any symbol which makes an inspirational statement.

- Make sure everyone contributes to the class banner. Combine some of the best ideas to represent the group.

- List "Words to Live By"

  Respect yourself–Support your classmates–Say a kind word daily–Make people feel good about themselves–Listen to each other–Lend a helping hand–Respect adults, etc.

For younger children, cut out magazine pictures which illustrate the concepts above. Mount on colorful construction paper. Attach to a wall or bulletin board or hang from a mobile. Discuss often.

TLC10080

Your Name Magazine

Through the weeks we will talk about many things that explain a great deal about your ideas, your personality, your interests and how you feel about yourself. You will begin to de-velop enough information about the kind of person you are so that you can put all that information in a magazine which is named after you!

Look at some magazines to see what information is included on the cover. Look inside for the Table of Contents and additional information. You may organize your contents in different ways such as: "Around School," "Around Home," "In the Neighborhood," "Hanging Out on the Town." To spark the interest of your reader, you may draw or cut out and paste small pictures next to some of the titles to illustrate the subject.

The rest is up to you. Through the weeks look for magazine pictures, advertisements and story titles that show something about you and your interests.

When the magazine is finished, it should give the reader a very clear idea of the kind of person you are inside and out! What activities and sports please you? What hobbies do you have? What are some things you would like to learn? What is your idea of a really great vacation? What makes you laugh? What makes you sad? What bothers you? What do you do to make your small universe a better place to live?

Because we are all complicated human beings, your magazine will never really be done–but when you finish the last page you will be astonished at how complex and interesting you are–and how much more there is to tell!

Your Name Magazine

Tender Loving Care Publishers

Date

Your City and State

Look carefully at several magazine covers for ideas. Use the details you like to make an attractive cover. Add some information on the outside cover that will give the reader a few clues about what's inside.

In the middle of the cover use a drawing of your face, your favorite snapshot or a scene or design of your choice.

Inside this issue:
- Trying Out for the Team
- Learning a Hard Lesson
- Recipes for Tough Cookies

Volume 4, Number 9
publication date
Your Name Magazine

TLC10080

Suggestions for a Table of Contents with Pictures

Friends I like
My name means
My most scary moment
What makes me mad!
Fun activities
Foods I love

If wishes came true

Favorite music

Places I like to go

The best story I know
What I want to learn
A joke or a riddle

People I admire
Something to brag about
Good and bad dreams
I will never forget
When I grow up
Why can't I . . .

My pet

Clothes I like to wear

A great movie
Work I like to do
My family
Hanging out

A gift I would like

My favorite game

Listen Up
A Poem from Teacher to Student

Be Kind to Yourself!
Never downgrade yourself
Never bad mouth yourself
Don't say, "I'm dumb"
Or "I'm just not smart enough"
Or "I can't do anything right!"

It doesn't help anyone to talk that way
Least of all you!

We are all trying for the same things:
    We want to be loved.
    We want to be good and do things well
    To have friends
    To find our way
        in school, at home,
        in our neighborhood.

However you measure yourself
Big or small–
There is a place for you in the stars
Each in our way leaves a special mark
One person can make a difference.

You had better believe that!

We will listen to your thoughts and feelings
    (What inspires you? What scares you?)
We will help you feel that you can do things
    well.
That you have some power and
    control in your life
That you are worthy of love and praise!

All of this will work its way
Into your heart and soul
To nurture your self-respect

And you will find your place in the
    stars and leave your special mark.

You had better believe that!

Greta B. Lipson

TLC10080

Tell Us Who You Are
Professor Covensky

Tell Us Who You Are
Professor Covensky

Once upon a time there was a very kind professor who was a teacher at Wayne State University in the city of Detroit. His name was Professor Covensky, and he taught the history of the entire world. His students were not in elemen- tary school or middle school; they were grown- ups who had gradu- ated from high school and were in college to become teachers, engineers, librarians, doctors, lawyers and other trained people.

Professor Covensky was an excit- ing teacher and students clamored to get into his class. As you might expect, he was friendly. He had a small gray beard and a sunshine smile set in a warm and welcoming face. But more important—every lesson he taught was another fascinating story to which his students listened in quiet amazement. He could take the part of kings and queens. He could be a poor peasant farmer in the field. He could be a general or a wounded soldier in a war! And often he used a pointer (as a make-believe threat) to select a student eager to play his game.

He told the students about long ago. He made them feel as if they were actually in those ancient countries when he explained about Egypt and China and other faraway places in the world. Best of all, the students felt comfortable and happy in his class- room.

One day he said, "I am going to ask you a serious question and if you can answer it, you will get an A+ in an instant. Then you will not have to do anything else in this class except come to class, read and lis- ten and help us discuss things."

As you can imagine, the students were very excited. They thought that answering the professor's question would be like solving a riddle. How hard could it be? One little question and they would have a good grade for the rest of the semester.

"First, you must all agree to this plan." Professor Covensky said, "If you like the offer, raise your hand." Every hand in the room went up. They waited to see what would happen next.

TLC10080

"May we hear the question now, Professor?" someone asked quietly.

Professor Covensky smiled, "Yes, of course." Looking straight at the students he said, "My question is: WHO ARE YOU?"

There was silence. The students couldn't believe their ears. What an easy question! All the hands shot up in the air. The professor looked around slowly and chose an especially smart girl. "Who are you?" he repeated.

"Who am I?" she cleared her throat, "I am Rosita Martinez," she answered happily.

"Is that who you are?" Professor Covensky asked.

"Yes," she said in a soft voice, not quite sure now.

"You are more than just a name," he said thoughtfully. "Your answer is not complete."

And so the weeks went by in Professor Covensky's class. Every day they met and every day the students racked their brains trying to answer his question: "Who are you?" Each time they thought of another way to answer, he would say, "You are more than that . . . ."

So it seemed that the good professor had an answer in his mind that no one could figure out. But as each person tried, it was clear that Professor Covensky believed that each and every one of his students was more than a name, more than an address, more than all the things they could describe about themselves.

With the magic of a great teacher, he helped us reflect about ourselves. He showed us, in a different way than ever before, how varied and valuable our roles in life really were. When his classroom door closed, it was as if we said to one another, "Here we are–together again, assembled for more thrills and chills."

A hush would fall, as if in a theater. Every meeting was a performance in which we all played our parts eagerly. That deep and mellow voice would come rolling out and we would

begin. He had a wonderfully resounding laugh and, to his credit, he was an attentive and thoughtful listener. Best of all, he made his students laugh! They laughed through weeks of hard work and adventure.

Once, when class was in session, the door opened and a ragtag fellow walked in playing mellow music on a saxophone. He made a turn around the room and just as quickly as he entered, he exited–leaving the class stunned with surprise. Professor Covensky had planned it to show how we each can see things differently.

He did good things for us. He respected us in the fullness and diversity of our backgrounds. He included us in our own learning. It wasn't just how much he knew--it was

the way he brought the stories of history to life that made us willing listeners.

Dr. Covensky would often close the hour with something for us to think about. His questions were as big as the universe, and we struggled to answer them. In a booming voice he would ask: "What is the greatest tragedy of all–the tragedy of ignorance (to be unaware) or–the tragedy of knowledge (to be aware but powerless to do anything about a situation)?" He made philosophers of us all.

The truth about this story is that I was in that very classroom learning and wondering (along with everyone else) what the answers to Professor Covensky's questions could be.

It was he who taught us that the influence of a great teacher goes on forever!

Perhaps, as you go through this book you can try to answer hard questions about yourself and come to appreciate all the things you are! While you are on this trip of discovery, we hope you will learn what makes you a special person, a valuable human being–and important in the lives of other people.

Tell Us Who You Are
Student Activities

- Use a challenging form called "Alphabetical Me" in which you describe yourself from A to Z! Write in complete sentences. Underline the letter you are using. Be honest but don't be modest. Help people learn more about you using the following example:

Alphabetical Me (from A to Z)
<u>A</u> I am crazy about making model airplanes.
<u>B</u> Some people call me a basketball freak.
<u>C</u> You can hear my voice in the chorus.
<u>D</u> My dog's name is Flapjack.
<u>E</u> I earn money cutting lawns on my street.

Challenge younger children to name something about themselves or their likes or dislikes for each letter of the alphabet. For example: Apples, Bouncing a ball, Curly hair, etc.

- Print your entire name, first and last in large letters. Use a different color for each letter. Decorate the strokes with symbols, leaves and curlicues. Frame your name with a border. Create a wild abstract design. This unique personal design will be part of a "Name Art Exhibit" for your classroom.

- Find a book of names in the library which lists names and their meanings. Use the book as a model, then make believe that your name was taken out of a very current volume. Give your name an interesting description. Think of things in nature or technology. Think of colors, talents and characteristics: Alexander (solar planner), Jill (rainbow in the sky), Eric (radio waves), Matthew (peacemaker), Susan (cyberspace jockey), Mark (celestial musician).

- Is your given name (first name) the same as a relative in your family? Ask at home how it came about. Do you have a nickname? Often these names have a strange or funny origin and sometimes they last for a lifetime. Is there a story behind yours?

- For a really funny experience, try writing or printing your name backwards! You must decide on the way you will pronounce it. (My complete name is Aterg Yalcrab Nospil)! We never make fun of a person's name, but this backwards name game is something to laugh about. Who is willing to pronounce his or her backwards name for the class? Is it a problem? If so, why?

- A collage is an artistic composition of materials and objects pasted on a surface. Look through magazines and cut out pictures of things, people and activities which express your interests and personality. Paste these pictures on colored construction paper and trim the entire composition in a pleasant free form. If you wish, you may attach this collage to a hanger to swing from an overhead wire. Explain your personal collage to your classmates.

- Create a name acrostic and try to capture the kind of person you are using the letters of your first name, last name or both. (This may also be a whole class effort with one name written on the chalkboard and suggestions from the group. It can be an exercise in positive descriptions of one's classmates).

18

Acrostics

Gerrie
Acrostic

GOOD
ENERGETIC
RELIABLE
RESPECTFUL
INTERESTING
EARNEST

Use your name with one word representing each letter or use each letter to develop descriptive phrases:

JUST A GOOD KID
ALWAYS READY TO PLAY BALL
CHECKERS IS MY GAME
KING OF THE PIZZA EATERS

- Make a chart out of your first, middle, last or nickname. Print your name at the top. Draw a graph chart under the name. You may use any categories that have possibilities with the letters of the name. See suggestions below. Because this is difficult, you may choose your own categories such as restaurants, creatures, clothing, flowers, athletes, colors, authors, etc. Explore the possibilities. Remember that each line must spell the name horizontally. The class may act as consultant for one another in case someone cannot come up with an idea.

For example:

	Beth			
Food	Bananas	Eggs	Toast	Hominy
Cities	Boston	El Paso	Toronto	Halifax
Games	Basketball	Egg toss	Tennis	Hockey
Cars	Buick	Europa	Taurus	Honda
Creatures	Bat	Eel	Tiger	Hippopotamus

Tell Us Who You Are

Student Page

Name: _____

> ## Professor Covensky

My thoughts about this story: _____

_____

_____

_____

_____

_____

_____

Draw a picture from this story.

TLC10080

You Are One of a Kind
Clotho and Her Sisters

You Are One of a Kind
*Clotho and Her Sisters**

The religion of the ancient Greeks included many gods whom, they believed, lived at the top of Mt. Olympus. Some of these gods and their children had specific jobs to do. Others just lay around being mischievous, troublesome and just plain ornery. Among the goddesses there were three sisters Clotho (**CLO THO**), Lachesis (luh **KEE** sis) and Atropos (**AT** ro pos) who worked seriously. These three sisters had magical powers. They were given only one important job to do every single day that affected the lives of human beings.

"We can't have people who are all alike in this world," they said. "That would be a terrible mess!" And so they set about making everyone's life different!

Before a child was born, the sisters would plan the pattern of each child's life. They decided that though some people might resemble others, no individual would be exactly like another! Each sister had a particular job as they wove the tapestry of every human life. They made a living quilt which told the story of each and every life. No one could tell them what to do or make them undo their work–not kings or queens or other gods with power.

Clotho was the spinner. She would spin the thread of life with light and dark lines. The light lines stood for happiness, and the dark lines stood for sadness. This meant that some people would be very lighthearted and smiling, while others always faced life with a frown on their faces.

Lachesis was the sister who twisted the threads. She made some of the threads weak and easy to pull apart which made that life frail and easy to break under strain. Some threads were twisted tight and thick which made that life very strong and tough!

Atropos was the last to work on the tapestry. She frightened everyone because it was her job to decide when the thread of life was to be cut. It was she who measured how long a person would live on this Earth. Sometimes she cut the thread short and sometimes long. When the sisters started and finished a job, they knew that every human life, like their tapestries, would have a different pattern. No one knew how they made their decisions. Now, as then, we can never know the secret of how each life will unfold.

*Clotho and her sisters were called "The Fates."

TLC10080

I Am One of a Kind

Two eyes
A chin
And hair that grows

Two ears
A mouth
A nose that blows

Eyebrows
Two cheeks
Two rows of teeth

Two arms
Good hands
Two sturdy feet

A piece of work
That can't be beat

A miracle!
Creation's feat!

In all the world
How can it be?
That no one else is just like me?

Greta B. Lipson

You Are One of a Kind
Student Activities

• There are all kinds of weavings made from a variety of materials. The following assignment will weave a poem from words that say something about you or other good people. This poem will not rhyme! In this way your poem will flow more easily and you will have more freedom to express yourself. You can write it alone or in a small group.

Choose four phrases from the 12 lyrical lines below. Add those borrowed lines to the beginning, the middle or the ending of four or more of your own lines. Find words that are meaningful to you. Add as many lines as you wish, or change a word here or there as long as the poem makes sense. This is hard to do, but just as is true among people– the variations can be amazing. When the poem is finished, read the final effort to the class.

Variations on a Theme

Borrow four of these lines:

a. My eyes look to the horizon
b. A patch of blue lifts my spirits
c. Come walk the gentle pathway
d. I am one of a kind in all the world
e. An honest person shows the way
f. If you want a friend, then be a friend
g. Pride shines bright from words of praise
h. I offer my gift of loyalty
i. Wisdom opens many doors
j. Kind deeds come back to you
k. Laughter is the music of joy
l. Smiles light up distant skies

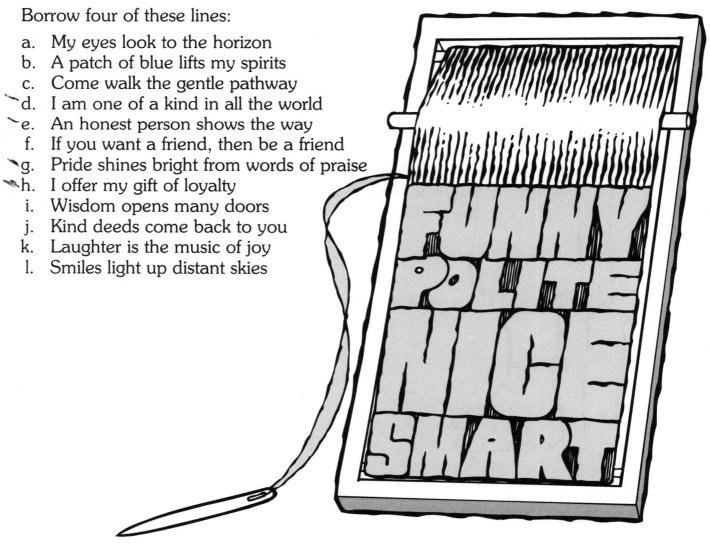

TLC10080

- You are going to make a one-of-a-kind, interesting recipe of yourself! Before you do this, have a class discussion about some of the terms that are used in recipes. The teacher may read some recipes to help everyone understand how cakes, cookies, stews and other foods are put together. The cooking terms may be listed on the chalkboard and expanded with imagination.

For example:

separate	blend	scramble	beat	chop	spice
measure	fry	puree	cream	sprinkle	frost
sift	broil	whip	fold	knead	pour

A Recipe of Me

1. Sift all-purpose flour with powerful amounts of baking powder for rising muscles. Add 3 cups (720 ml) of sugar for lots of sweetness. Mix in some melted butter for a soft heart and a pinch of cinnamon for freckles. Stir in red food coloring for a headful of wild hair. Add almonds for a mouthful of big teeth. Bake well until tender feelings form.

2. Mix together a bag of marsh-mallows and brown eyes. Add short black hair and lips that are always moving. Blend a quick brain and a good heart. Fold in chocolate skin and a firm jaw. Whip up a big bowl of personality and mix to make a really neat kid.

- Your fingerprints are one of a kind! Your prints are made by the ridges found on your fingers and thumbs. Believe it or not–there has never been a record of any two people having identical prints. For that reason, fingerprints are an absolute means of identification. Prepare to take your own prints by using an ink pad. Press your finger and/or thumb onto the pad, and then press your finger carefully onto a white piece of paper. For more fun, have the prints enlarged on a copy machine and study the differences you see. Be sure your name is at the top of the paper.

- Imagine that there is only one of you in a world population of about 5 billion, 734 million (5,734,000,000). Find the latest population figures for this year! In the book, *Where's Waldo*, by Martin Handford (© 1987, published by Little Brown), we look for Waldo on every page as he hikes all over the world and invites the reader to find his face in every crowded place to which he travels. Draw a similar picture, tightly packed with people. Place your own singular smiling face shining out of the crowd and title the picture, "I Am One of a Kind." It will take a long time to complete and color, but you may work on it a bit at a time.

- Our English word *cloth* is named after the ancient Greek goddess Clotho, the spinner. In olden times cloth was produced on a loom, by interweaving thread or yarn. You can make a paper weaving according to the following directions.

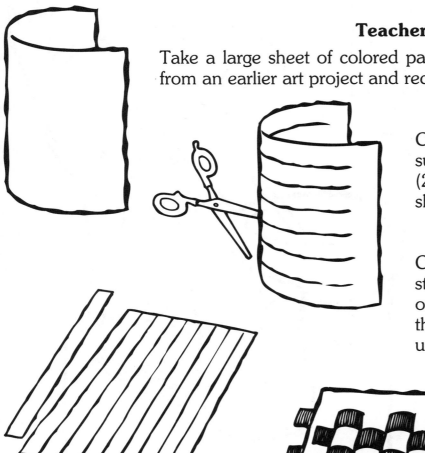

Teacher Directions

Take a large sheet of colored paper (it could be "previously colored" from an earlier art project and recycled) and fold in half.

Cut slits along the folded edge, making sure the slits only come to within 1" (2.5 cm) of the open edges. The slits should be about 1" (2.5 cm) apart.

Cut another sheet of colored paper into strips (try a variety of widths, tear out or cut out with pinking shears). Thread through the big slit paper, in an over-under pattern, as shown.

Laminate when finished and use for a place mat or book cover.

TLC10080

You Are One of a Kind

Student Page   **Name:** _____

> ## Clotho and Her Sisters

My thoughts about this story: _____

_____

_____

_____

_____

_____

_____

Draw a picture from this story.

Be Kind and You Will Receive Kindness
Androcles and the Lion

TLC10080

Be Kind and You Will Receive Kindness
Androcles and the Lion

All the rich households in ancient Rome kept slaves to cook and clean and attend to the daily needs of the families. In one of these households there was a slave whose name was Androcles (An-dro-kleez) who was treated very badly. His master was cruel. He beat Androcles daily until the poor servant could stand it no longer.

At the first opportunity, Androcles ran away. It was a dangerous decision since he had no money and no place of safety to go. If he were found he would certainly be put to death as a runaway slave. Frightened, he headed for the dark woods hoping for the safety of the tall trees and the thick underbrush. Once there, he realized that he would soon starve to death without food and water.

Androcles grew weak and sick. Finally, no longer able to walk upright, he found a cave. He crawled into its cool darkness certain that this place would be his last haven. He fell into a deep, sleep and dreamed he heard a frightening roar. But it wasn't a dream. He awoke, his heart beating wildly—as in the dim light he saw, to his horror,

a huge lion in the cave with him. The creature, roaring with pain, had crawled in bleeding from a wound.

The lion paid no attention to the man. Androcles stayed quite still, trying to figure out the danger of the situation. He was certain that the moment the animal saw a man in the cave it would attack him. But the powerful beast was in a sorry state and was biting desperately at his front paw. Androcles could see that there was a huge thorn deep into the lion's foot. Cautiously the man stepped forward, slowly, slowly and touched the injured paw.

TLC10080

It was as if the lion understood that this silent, good man would help him. The thorn was easy to see and Androcles grabbed it with his fingers and pulled it out as quickly as he could. The lion let out a frightening roar and then began to lick his wound to ease the pain.

Androcles did not move, still frightened and afraid, when the lion rubbed his head on the man's shoulder. The man stopped and then tenderly patted the lion's mane. The man felt that he had nothing to fear. That night they slept in the cave together–man and beast warming each other with kindness.

Came the dawn of a new day and the lion led the man to a clear stream for water. He brought food to the hungry man for many days after. The animal ate his meat raw and watched as Androcles cooked his meat over an open fire. They became devoted and loving friends. The man grew stronger and was ever grateful to his wild friend, until one day their sweet adventure ended. Androcles was discovered by the emperor's soldiers. They arrested him and dragged him in chains to the city where he was sure to be put to death. He never knew what became of his lion friend.

There was a custom in those times that runaway slaves were to be part of a great sports event in the coliseum. The coliseum was the place where spectator sport was open to the public to satisfy their pleasure and appetite for violence. It was a huge stadium, much like our football fields of today. It was not expected that the participants would ever leave the field! This was the place where lions would fight men to the death to the delight of the crowd.

TLC10080

The animals were locked up and starved to make them more ferocious. It was brutal and the crowd loved it. It was their circus, their fun, their entertainment!

The Emperor sat in his royal box in the front, carefully protected from the beasts. His was the very best seat in the arena so that he could see the terror on the faces of the miserable creatures (man and beast). Androcles was the first on the program. He was given a club–a small stick with which to fight a crazed and hungry lion. He was in despair and hoped his end would come quickly.

The gate to the lions' holding pit opened and a powerful lion came bounding out, hungry and angry. He was at the side of Androcles in seconds and all at once--to the bewilderment of the shouting spectators, the lion stopped--licked the hands of the terrified slave and rubbed his mane against the man's legs! It was a moment of gentle recog-

nition when Androcles realized the lion was his old friend.

The blood-thirsty crowd demanded to know why they were cheated out of their violent show! The emperor summoned Androcles to his box. "Tell me, slave! What is this? Did you do this with magic? Are you a wizard? I am waiting for your answer."

Androcles explained, "When I was beyond hope, this wild beast saved me. I did a small favor for him, and he responded with more goodness than I have ever been shown by men. He saved my life and is my friend of the heart."

The emperor was deeply moved by this story of kindness on the part of both man and beast. He stood in all his majesty and said, "I decree on this day that both slave and beast be set free in Rome to live together in peace and safety for the rest of their natural lives."

And so they did.

Be Kind and You Will Receive Kindness
Student Activities

> To feel "proud" means that you are pleased with yourself because you did something special. You may have solved a hard problem, learned a new game, done a favor for a friend, helped someone at home or given comfort to an animal. If you were to keep track of the many things that make you feel proud, you would not only be amazed but would impress others as being a very special person.

- Look up the word *pride* in the dictionary. Post a piece of butcher paper in class to record significant weekly good deeds of class members which are a source of pride. Discuss the kinds of actions that give you a sense of satisfaction and self-respect.

- Look for an impressive true story in the news, about someone who did something exceptional. Search for a fictional story about someone's unexpected kindness or heroism which impressed you. Organize a story fest in which class members tell stories of courage. These stories may be small or on a grand scale. Give the source of your story.

- Design some medals and decorations that can be pinned to a shirt or hung around the neck as an award of honor. Label these appropriately so that others will know at a glance what this symbol of excellence stands for. Use aluminum foil, sparkles, fancy buttons or anything decorative to catch the eye.

- Write a paragraph entitled "My Proudest Moment." Think back to a special event in your life when something made you feel great about yourself. The author, Robert Cormier, who wrote *The Chocolate War* and other teenage favorites, once explained to an audience about such a moment when, as a fourth grader, his teacher read his essay and said, emphatically, "Robert, you are a writer!" She could have said, "That's a good paper" or "what a nice job," but it wouldn't have meant the same.

- There are many people in our lives who do kind things for us every day. Whenever you say "thank you," it always makes them feel especially good! Think of someone special, a friend or grown-up to whom you could send a thank-you note. Use construction paper and fold it to look like a greeting card. Use markers, crayons, stickers and whatever else you think will make your card special. On the cover print, *Thank You*. Inside the card compose a simple sentence to express your appreciation to that special person. Kind words mean a great deal for the spirit, and they do not cost anything! Remember to sign your name.

A True Vignette
The Heimlich Maneuver
A Young Child's Heroism

The Heimlich maneuver is a technique named after the American surgeon, Dr. Henry J. Heimlich who was born in 1920. This first aid emergency technique is used to clear an object such as food, from the trachea (windpipe) of a choking person. The technique employs a firm upper thrust just below the rib cage. This pressure forces air out of the victim's lungs and blows the blockage from the windpipe so that normal breathing can take place again.

Some years ago the following story was reported in the newspapers:

There were two little neighbors, a boy, who was seven and a girl, who was six. They were very good friends and played together all the time. One afternoon they were sitting next to one another on the floor watching television when the little girl popped a butterscotch candy into her mouth and started to choke on it!

The boy had seen a program called *Rescue 911*, in which they demonstrated the Heimlich maneuver which was used to save the life of a choking person. He learned the lesson well, and he sprang into action doing all the things for his little friend which he had seen done on the program.

He stood behind her and put his arms tightly around her waist, high under her ribs. He squeezed hard around her abdomen once--twice--and three times which forced her to cough hard and presto--she coughed up the butterscotch candy and it flew out of her mouth.

The boy actually saved the little girl's life by performing the maneuver. When asked how she felt about her smart seven-year-old friend who had rescued her, her comment was, "He's my hero and I love him, but I won't let him kiss me!"

Be Kind and You Will Receive Kindness

Student Page

Name: _____

Androcles and the Lion

My thoughts about this story: _____

_____

_____

_____

_____

_____

_____

Draw a picture from this story.

Choose Your Friends Wisely
Cat and Mouse in Partnership

Choose Your Friends Wisely

Cat and Mouse in Partnership

Sometimes perfectly smart people choose the wrong friends. You usually know when you are in bad company and when it's time to find different companions! We are all judged by the company we keep, so be sure you can be proud of the people in your circle of friends.

This brings us to the odd friendship between Marcy Mouse and Alley Cat. They met on a day when the fall wind was blowing the leaves off the trees and the days were growing colder. Both of them were worried about finding a warm winter shelter and putting enough food away for the long cold days ahead. These two unlikely creatures had a friendly conversation, and Alley Cat said to the hardworking little Marcy Mouse, "What do you say about living together this coming winter? It would be a good plan for both of us."

Marcy Mouse was a trusting soul who considered this plan seriously. Besides that, Alley Cat was really very handsome and spoke very nicely. So Marcy agreed, "It sounds like a fine plan to me. I could take care of our home and you, who are a strong hunter, could go out and find food. As friends, we could be a good team."

The friends of Marcy Mouse couldn't believe their ears. "You are not using your head," they all said. "You know Alley Cat is not to be trusted. He is tough and has always taken what he wanted without thinking of others. He could be a great danger to you. Nobody has a good word to say about Alley Cat. Think about some of the bad things he's done. Please give this more thought."

Have you ever had a discussion in which you felt that you were right and everyone else was wrong? Nothing Marcy Mouse's friends said could convince her that she had made a poor choice of a friend.

Her only reply was, "But he is so good looking! Just being with him gives me the feeling that we will be happy together and our lives will be good. He is strong and smart--what could possibly go wrong?"

And so the two moved in together. The first exciting thing that happened was that Marcy Mouse found a big pot of fat which could be used for food if things got hard through the winter. They hid this potful in a secret place in the local church, away from other animals who might eat it. They promised each other that they would eat from the pot only in case of emergency.

36

The winter was harsher than expected, and the snow and ice covered their little home. They were warm and safe, it is true, but it made hunting for food a most difficult task. Each day Alley Cat would leave and come back with almost nothing to eat! But he seemed very content and would curl up in front of their fireplace, lick his lips, clean his whiskers and fall into a deep sleep. Marcy Mouse made the best of things, but it was hard with so little to eat.

One evening, as Alley Cat was fast asleep, snoring, Marcy Mouse thought it was time to dip into the pot of fat and bring some home for both of them. It would be a grand supper and would celebrate the success of their plan. She tiptoed out with a bowl and a lid and went to the church. When she arrived at the hiding place, the pot was almost completely empty and all around it were fatty paw prints!

She knew then that the cat had come every day to eat his fill!

Marcy Mouse was ready to scold Alley Cat, and she burst into the house angrily and started shouting! "You are dishonest. You broke your promise to me that we would work together and share our food and have an honest friendship. Now, what is to become of us with no food to help us through this long cold winter?"

Alley Cat rose from his comfortable place by the fire. He stretched to his full length, and his beautiful coat shone in the firelight. She had never seen him look more handsome or dangerous. He spoke slowly with a voice that was thick and heavy. "I don't know about you, Marcy dear, but I don't have to worry about my next delicious meal. I know just where it will come from! And can you believe it–I don't even have to leave home to get it."

Choose Your Friends Wisely
Student Activities

- You are judged by the friends you make. What does your choice of friends say about you? What does your choice of friends say about how you feel about yourself?

- What must you do to make and keep a friend? As a class, contribute to some ideas listed on the chalkboard.

    How to Make a Friend   How to Keep a Friend   How to Lose a Friend

- Organize into small groups. Discuss the meaning of friends. Choose someone to write everyone's definition in short phrases. Then decide on the best six lines and put them together in any order for the best sound and meaning. For example, start with:

A FRIEND IS . . .
always there for me
around in good times and bad
a person who shares
a pal who truly listens
a partner in tears and laughter
someone who respects me!

THAT IS A FRIEND!

- Sometimes when we read a story we meet a character who seems so wonderful, exciting or good-hearted that we wish that he or she were genuinely real. If such a character could step out of a story and step into your life as a friend, who would it be? Explain your choice to the class. Give the title and author of the book. Can you answer some questions about the person you have chosen?

- What if you had to write a note to a pal to say that in your opinion, he or she had just made a bad choice of a friend? You must be careful and use good judgement so that you do not hurt feelings. What would you write?

- In small groups, conduct a library search to find some of the many quotes about friends and friendship. Discuss your research with your librarian. (Ask to see Familiar Quotations by John Bartlett and similar volumes.) Devote a bulletin board to these sayings and include the author, if known, and the date (which may surprise you). The following quote (slightly modernized) by George Herbert is from the 17th century: "He that lies down with dogs rises with fleas." What do you think that means?

For the teacher's pleasure: Shakespeare wrote in Richard II, "I count myself in nothing else so happy/As in a soul remb'ring my good friends.")

- Make a string of paper dolls to represent your friends. Write the name of each friend on the body. Try to explain why you value these people. Why do you think friends are important?

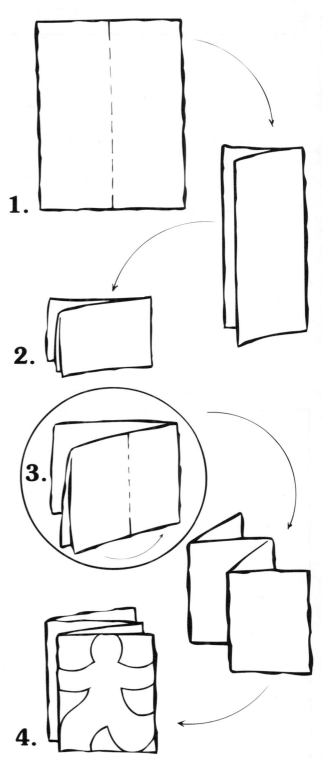

Making Four Paper Dolls

Teacher Directions

1. Take an 8½" x 11" (22 x 28 cm) sheet of paper and fold in half the long way.

2. Then fold in half again.

3. And again, bringing open edges to folded edge.

4. Then cut or tear so at least ¼ of the folded edge remains in order for it to stand up.

Choose Your Friends Wisely

Student Page   **Name:** _____

> *Cat and Mouse in Partnership*

My thoughts about this story: _____

_____

_____

_____

_____

_____

_____

Draw a picture from this story.

Happiness Comes from Within
The Shirt Off His Back

Happiness Comes from Within
The Shirt Off His Back*

Once there was a king who had only one son whom he named Cosmos. He loved the boy with all his heart, but there was one serious problem! The king could never make his boy happy. Cosmos had everything a person could wish for but he never smiled, he never laughed, and what was even worse--he was not interested in anything at all.

Cosmos would stare out the window for hours and say nothing. Once in a while he would sigh, with a great deep sound that came from the very bottom of his soul and escaped through his mouth!

The king would look into his son's eyes and ask, "Do you want to marry the most beautiful woman in the world? Shall we have a wonderful costume party and invite the most interesting people in the kingdom? Would you like to plan the most exciting music festival ever?"

The answer was always the same: "No, Father."

As you might guess, the king was set on doing something about this terribly sad situation because, like any parent, he only wanted happiness for his child. The king sent out the news that he needed the help of philosophers, physicians and great thinkers who might know how to make his son happy. The great thinkers came from all over the kingdom. They examined Cosmos. They listened to his heartbeat and his stomach gurgling. They talked to him. They looked him over from head to toe and then they sat down to talk it over! Finally the wise ones said, "Your majesty, we think we've got it."

The king listened with a heavy heart as they spoke. "Find a thoroughly happy man—a person who is pleased with his life and is happy through and through! Buy his shirt to put on your son! We believe that such a shirt will be the answer to your problem!"

*Adapted from Italian Folktales by Italo Calvino.

TLC10080

The king's messengers found a priest, a nobleman, a merchant and an artist--but unfortunately, each in his own way was not completely happy. The priest wanted to be a bishop. The nobleman wanted more land. The merchant needed a ship that would sail to faraway places, and the artist wished that more people would buy his paintings!

The king worried about his son whose face grew sickly as time passed. One miserable, gray day, as the king walked in the woods surrounding the palace, he heard a man singing as if his heart were soaring with joy. The king came closer and saw that the joyous voice came from a young peasant who worked on the king's own land. He worked with such pleasure that every bone in his body showed his happiness at being alive.

"At last! At last my son will be saved," the king shouted as he came toward the lad. He was certain that he would find this young person to be completely happy with his life! Of course the king had to ask the young fellow some questions. "Are you happy with your life, young man?"

"Oh yes, your majesty. My life is wonderful! I am blessed with a loving family, with good health and honorable friends."

"Wouldn't you rather come with me and live the life of a nobleman in my palace? You could live in luxury, wear the finest clothes, eat the best food and not work at all for the rest of your life." The king, of course, was testing the young peasant.

"Oh no," the young man replied, "I would not care to trade places with the highest lord in the land! I am perfectly happy and content with my life just as it is!"

"At last my search is over," said the king. "Now I will be able to make my son happy." He walked over to the young peasant and asked, "Please, young sir, please give me your shirt. I will give you any price you ask if only I can have the shirt off your back to save my son."

"I would be most honored to help you, your kind majesty, but I fear I must refuse. I cannot help you."

The king was angry now and shouted. "You ungrateful scamp! How can you refuse me? Where is your heart? Give me a reason why you will not sell me your shirt!"

The happy peasant opened up his jacket so the king might see, "Because my lord--I am not wearing a shirt!"

Happiness Comes from Within
Student Activities

- The meeting of the wise people, whom the king called together to help his son, is being held in your classroom. Ask for volunteers to playact this meeting. What is each person's point of view? The king has selected one citizen to ask the wise people questions and conduct the assembly. Everyone does not agree on a solution for the young prince. After listening to the discussion, the class may talk to the participants, disagree or discuss some attitudes.

- About shirts: sports stars, movie actors, musicians and all kinds of famous people have their names on T-shirts and sweatshirts. It's about time that somebody thought about ordinary, everyday good people who deserve recognition, too! Think of a design and a statement that can be printed on a T-shirt that tells the world about your good character. For example: Just Plain Nice, Good Listener, Deep Thinker, Book Worm, Strong and Silent, Stamp Saver, Dependable, True Pal, Animal Lover, Environmentalist.

- People, young or old, cannot always laugh and smile every minute. There are sad moments and down times when things are not going well and you may feel troubled. As a class discuss the ways students can help themselves or ask for help. Invite the school social worker or school psychologist to your class to address these issues. Prepare unsigned questions for the "expert" to respond to and to foster discussion.

- Some people, when they are "down in the dumps" or stressed out, make a trip to the kitchen for a favorite "comfort" food that makes them feel better. Maybe it's a cup of hot chocolate with a marshmallow bobbing around or chicken noodle soup or a bowl of popcorn to lift the spirits. What is your comfort food? Write a one-page uplifting recipe. Collect the papers and put them together to look like a prescription pad.

- Design your very own happy face (or sad face) on a white T-shirt which you bring from home (an old one is just fine). The best results will be obtained from a shirt that is at least 50% polyester. The higher the polyester content, the more vivid and lasting the design will be. The teacher will supply fabric crayons in an assortment of colors, which are available in fabric stores. Practice on paper first, and if your school is lucky enough to have an art teacher, ask him or her for expert help.

- Drama is a form of storytelling in which there are actors who act out a story on the stage or in the movies. Since ancient times people have been entertained by stories that make them laugh and cry. The happy mask and sad masks, side-by-side, are used as a symbol of drama in real life. Using a supermarket bag, make a bold happy face on one side and a really downhearted face on the other side. Write a thoughtful statement under each mask.

Happiness Comes from Within

Student Page   **Name:** _____

> ### The Shirt Off His Back

My thoughts about this story: _____

_____

_____

_____

_____

_____

_____

Draw a picture from this story.

TLC10080

People Are Beautiful Because We Love Them
A Crack in the Wall

People Are Beautiful Because We Love Them
A Crack in the Wall*

> We do not love people because they are beautiful, but they seem beautiful to us because we love them.
> –An old Russian proverb

No one had ever wanted a baby girl more than Lord and Lady Heavenrich! When their dear infant was born, they were very, very happy. They named her Daphne because she had arrived when the first daffodils burst into bloom in May.

Her mother and father believed that no one had ever seen such a child. She was quick and sweet and she smiled at everyone, whether they were servants or noble people. Her parents wanted only the very best for little Daphne, but they were afraid that some harm might befall, her so they made a strange plan. They decided, out of love, to build a stone wall around their child to protect her. Stone by stone the wall grew higher and higher as her barrier from the world was finished.

Sometimes people believe that miracles only happen to them alone. It never occurred to

Lord and Lady Heavenrich that right next door to their castle the very same story had just taken place. Their neighbors, Lord and Lady Angelhair, had just welcomed their own special wonder child whom they named Norbert Angelhair! He was a little boy of such charm that they spent their days gazing upon the beautiful features of this dark-haired little lad.

Like all parents, Lord and Lady Angelhair wanted baby Norbert to have a happy childhood, but they knew that his handsomeness would make that impossible. After talking it over, the Angelhairs had an imposing stone wall built to enclose their precious child to hide him from admiring eyes and too much public flattery.

*From Only a Mother Could Love You by G.B. Lipson, © 1985.

TLC10080

Because the families had built the walls so close together there came to be a place where the walls fused and became as one. The children, Daphne and Norbert, who were now grown, played in their own separate gardens. Each had a favorite place to hug the wall where the sun warmed their faces and shone brightly on the climbing morning glory.

Sadly each child felt lonely, for there was never another to play with or talk to. It was perhaps true that these beautiful children had to be protected from prying eyes, but what a price to pay!

Now it happened that one day Daphne was standing in her garden, singing a little song she had made up. She sang as she scratched busily at a stone in the wall:

> We haven't even met just yet
> When will you pass this way?
> The hours drag with no one here.
> I long for us to play.
>
> We'll sing to the sun in the morning
> And croon to the moon at night
> And fill the hours in between
> With laughter and delight.
>
> When will you pass this way?
> When will you come to play?
> When will you fill each quiet hour
> And share my lonely day?

Norbert, in his garden, heard that sweet song through the wall. His heart began to pound. He stopped and was as still as a frightened mouse, as he listened to each word. Mustering all his courage, he sang back softly.

> We'll sing to the sun in the morning
> And croon to the moon at night
> And fill the hours in between
> With laughter and delight.

That is the way it happened that the two children, beautiful Daphne and handsome Norbert, discovered one another. Slowly each of them picked away at the stones in the wall until they managed an opening that made it possible for their voices to be heard as clear as crystal. They were able to share in ways they never thought possible. How desperately they envied the birds who could visit both gardens with total freedom!

With each passing day they discovered how much alike they were. They told each other secrets. Daphne was very smart and Norbert was very clever, and they shared all that they had learned from books and from nature. They talked for hours through the wall and, as you might guess, they became the very best of friends!

They learned, as they grew closer, that both of them were too beautiful for the world of ordinary people. Strange as it may seem, each set of parents never allowed any mirrors to be given the children. Though neither Daphne nor Norbert had ever seen themselves, they knew from conversations

between their parents that they were beautiful beyond imagination. But still they could not see each other!

Norbert asked his mother, "Please tell me what I look like." Since she loved to describe him, she said, "Your hair is bluish-black like the feathers of the raven, and your fine features are princely and handsome."

Daphne asked her father, "Please tell me what I look like." Since he loved to describe his daughter, he said, "Your hair is soft and flaxen, your eyes are the color of the sea and you are straight as a cornflower." And so they repeated these things they had been told and both had beautiful images of the other.

It came to pass that where each child had dug away, the old wall began to crumble. Daphne and Norbert realized it would soon be possible to pass through an opening in the wall. The day arrived and each hurried to the garden to force the stones away.

After years of friendship they stood before one another speechless!

50

"You are a little blimp," exclaimed Daphne.

"You are a scrawny beanpole!" Norbert cried.

"You look like a dumpling with eyes," Daphne lamented.

"A strong wind could break you in two!

Who told you that you were a raving beauty?" Norbert demanded.

"My father told me," she responded.

"He lied!" Norbert said.

"And who gave you the idea that you were handsome?" Daphne demanded.

"My mother told me," he shouted.

"She was badly mistaken," Daphne grumbled.

"How could they? Why would they? What's the matter with those grown-ups?" Norbert cried into the wind.

"Because, you ninny–" Daphne explained, "they are our parents!"

These two stood, toe to toe, looking at each other for a very long time. There was no more shouting or carrying on. Now they were serious and quiet. They thought very hard.

"You are my very best friend in all the world," said the girl as skinny as a beanpole. "And you are my only true friend in all the world," said the boy who looked like a dumpling--as he held out his hand.

Their fingers locked in a bond of everlasting friendship. They turned their smiling faces up to the glorious blue sky as one and sang in unison:

Oh we'll sing to the sun in the morning
And croon to the moon at night
And fill the hours in between
With laughter and delight.

People Are Beautiful Because We Love Them
Student Activities

- Start a whole-class exercise that begins with the phrase: "Beauty is . . ." The teacher may model this exercise on the chalkboard by taking the first turn at defining beauty. Students can write their own definitions following the class activity. (Beauty is watching an entire class working together.)

- Explain one or more of the following phrases. Do you agree or disagree? Explain.
  - Beauty is only skin deep.
  - Beauty is in the eye of the beholder.
  - What is beautiful is invisible to the eye.
  - Beware of judging people by appearance alone.

- If you did not have the gift of sight, what qualities would you want to find in a good friend? Do you think it would be easier to judge a friend this way than if you could see his or her face? Why?

- If members of your class volunteered to help physically challenged kids in your school district, what effect could it have on the attitudes of your volunteer classmates? (Might it give them a new appreciation of their own good luck–and make them less likely to complain?)

- Even if you don't own a cat or dog it is easy to understand the deep love between pets and people. The pets can be funny looking and so can their owners, but still there is a lasting bond between them unlike any other. Reflect (in discussion or writing) upon this kind of devotion which has nothing whatsoever to do with good looks!

TLC10080

- The author, Jane Yolen, has written a story entitled *Sleeping Ugly*, © 1981, Putnam Group. Remember, Sleeping Beauty? This story is about Princess Miserella who is mean, nasty and rotten–but oh so beautiful! There is another character, Plain Jane, who is homely but so sweet that *everybody* loves her. She lives in a house that is so awful " . . . that the floor sank, the walls stank, and the roof leaked even on sunny days." There is, of course, a handsome prince, a little old fairy in disguise and an enchanted nap. The prince is destined to awaken someone with a kiss and fall in love! What happens to the nasty Princess Miserella? There is a surprise ending. Write your own ending and try to find this book in the library! (The Prince kisses Plain Jane first and falls in love with her sweetness. Princess Miserella continues to doze in her 100-year sleep and is kept upright in the house and used as a coatrack. The good fairy lives near the happy couple.)

- In this story the children cared for each other because of the kind of people they were on the inside. They both had "inner beauty." Create a class photo exhibit on your bulletin board. Bring in pictures of friends and family whom you care about deeply because of their inside beauty. Discuss a title for this important day. Vote on the title you think is best and use it as a header in large print.

Remember the following:
"What is essential is invisible to the eye," a quote from *The Little Prince* by Antonie de Saint-Exupery, © 1943, Harcourt Brace Jovanovich. The teacher may want to read this book to the students as well.

My Mother Is the Most Beautiful Woman in the World

A Russian folktale by Becky Reyher,
© 1986, Lothrop Lee & Shepard Books, New York

Synopsis

There is a Russian folktale which explains the ideal of loving a person, not for physical beauty, but for the goodness that resides inside of them: Varya, a little Russian peasant girl, went out into the fields daily with her mother and played happily in the tall wheat during harvesttime. One day, exhausted from the summer sun, little Varya fell into a deep sleep. When she awoke her mother was nowhere in sight! Frightened and lost, she went to some of the farmers and asked if they had seen her mother. When they asked what her mother looked like, she said, "My mother is the most beautiful woman in the world." They ran to the villages and rounded up the most beautiful women in the countryside--but her mother was nowhere among them! Finally, when the hour grew late, a frantic woman came dashing through the crowd and scooped up the little girl. It was Varya's mother, who covered her face with kisses! To everyone's surprise, the woman had a very ordinary face--plain in every respect. She was large and heavy and had a space in front where a tooth belonged. No--she was not beautiful in the least, but everyone understood that she seemed beautiful to her adoring child who loved her so very much.

Have you ever had an experience that would help you understand the meaning of this story more completely?

54

TLC10080

People Are Beautiful Because We Love Them

Student Page

Name: _____

A Crack in the Wall

My thoughts about this story: _____

_____

_____

_____

_____

_____

_____

Draw a picture from this story.

You Are a Fine Creation
The Belly and Its Members

TLC10080

You Are a Fine Creation
The Belly and Its Members*

> *What a noble piece of work is man . . .* —William Shakespeare

A long time ago, before any of us can remember, the body parts did not work very well together. They grumbled and complained a great deal. They all had separate jobs to do and felt put upon because they all had to feed the belly as well.

"How unfair!" they thought. "We spend so much of our precious day gathering all kinds of goodies and tasty food for the belly that we barely have enough time for ourselves," grumbled the hands and arms.

"You are not the only ones, you know," protested the legs. "If it were not for walking around and about all over the land, you would have nothing to gather to feed that lazy belly!"

"And do none of you consider that it is I--this pair of eyes--that shows you the way to all the places you walk to and all that food you gather to feed the belly?"

"Well!" said the mouth loudly, announcing his importance, "Where would the lot of you be without me to bite the food with my teeth and work it around with my tongue and send it on its way to the belly?"

But alas, no one answered anyone. They were all quite angry with these services which they performed for the belly.

"As far as I can see, the belly is a no-account, lazy, do-nothing," said the eyes, joined by the others.

"Nobody has ever thank-ed me for all the hard work I've done," fumed the lungs.

"He can't even say a word without me," said the tongue.

"Let him just hang in there," they all complained.

And so they talked things over among themselves and came to a firm decision. No longer would they be fools and contribute to this lazy belly. He did nothing in return, and they had had enough.

"You can depend upon me. No more seeking out food by looking this way and that," said the eyes.

"I'm through walking over hill and dale to do this thankless job," said the legs.

"And you won't catch me gathering," said the arms.

"Nor pushing food in," said the hands with disgust.

"If ever I take another morsel in," said the mouth, "I hope all my teeth rot and fall out."

And so these body parts foolishly thinking themselves all to be independent, held to their promises and none of them--not one--fed the belly! It is easy to imagine what happened. The lack of food in the belly made the arms grow thin and weak. They could barely hold the weight of the body. Arms and hands, too, were near to the bone, and the muscles withered and could not work. The eyes were cloudy with fever and weakness and could not view the world with any clearness of sight. Even the mouth, now sunken and silent, could hardly move.

The poor weakened members assembled in a circle for a meeting.

Oh, but they looked to be a sorry lot! Their voices were just whispers.

"It is good that you are all here, dear friends," whispered the mouth, opening the meeting.

"I fear we have been mistaken," said another.

"We have judged our situation wrongly."

"Surely this proves that we cannot all go our separate ways."

"All of us must help one another for our health and the good of all."

"Clearly, we depend upon one another for our very existence."

"The belly is slow and quiet, except when it gurgles, but still it does an important job to help keep us alive."

"This proves that each of us needs the others, and we must all work together."

And they did—as they all joined in a body for the common good.

You Are a Fine Creation
Student Activities

It is essential to understand and respect yourself as an important human being. Included in that understanding is learning how to value and protect the body. You make decisions every day that affect your body which is yours and yours alone for all the years ahead. The ways in which you learn to take care of yourself ensure your physical health. The things you eat, your cleanliness and the rituals that you practice all help to prevent disease. You are in charge of yourself for your entire life.

- There are many proverbs or sayings that have to do with the human body. An old favorite is from an unknown source: "If you don't take care of your body, where will you live?" or "Your body is a temple--so be a good caretaker" or "Your body's not a car. There are no trade-ins." (Or from Shakespeare [loosely]: "Our bodies are our gardens and we are the gardeners.") Make up some sayings that are reminders that the human body is a gift which must be cared for.

- Visit your library and find books that detail amazing facts about the human body and how it works. In groups, organize your information and develop a game, quiz or creative catalog of fascinating information. Give the project a catchy name, such as "What's Its Job?" Humorous cartoons would help! For example:
  - The heart is a muscle. How hard does it work? (An adult heart beats over 100,000 times a day throughout an entire lifetime.)
  - Why do we have skin? (It is like a stretchy suit that holds in and protects your insides.)
  - What do lungs do? (You breathe air in and the lungs take out the oxygen the body needs to make your muscles work.)
  - Why is the liver called the body's chemical factory? (Because it does at least 500 jobs for the body.)
  - What is the job of the two kidneys in the body? (They filter the blood and get rid of waste. The body is 70% water.)
  - What part of your body works like a computer with a fantastic memory? (The brain is your body's control center.)
  - How does a skeleton help the body? (It holds everything up and protects everything like a big framework.)
  - The human body is made up of cells which are building blocks. How many are there in an adult body? (About 50 billion which can only be seen under a microscope!)

59

- Anatomy describes the structure of your body. Physiology describes the ways in which your body functions. Read some general information about the human body from question and answer books. Divide into two teams and try to define, simply the body's systems and functions:

    Circulatory System
    Digestive System
    Nervous System
    Reproductive System
    Respiratory System
    Skeletal and Muscular Systems

- Invite the school nurse or a nurse from the Board of Health into your classroom. As you would do for any guest speaker, prepare good questions to ask that relate to the effects of drugs, alcohol and tobacco on the human body. Ask the nurse to bring a plastic anatomical form of the human body which can be taken apart, piece by piece.

- The heart is a part of the human body which is celebrated in songs, poetry and statements we make every day. Perhaps you have heard people say, "I love you with all my heart" or "Have a heart and help out" or "My heart is full of joy." The heart is used in language to express happiness, greatness, sadness, compassion and many human emotions. Down through the ages, love has been expressed with a picture of a heart which everyone understands in every language. Draw and cut out a large heart from construction paper. Print the words for love in other languages as follows:

French–amour	Arabic–houb	Danish–elskov
Polish–milosc	Greek–asa'pi	Italian–amore
Russian–lyubof	Spanish–amor	Japanese–ai
Swahili–upendo	Hebrew–ahavah	Czech–laska
German–liebe		

Ask at home for the word for *love* in other language groups.

60

A pantoum is a poetic form which does not rhyme. Create and number the lines that express your thoughts in your best dramatic style. The lines of poetry are repeated according to the pattern below. Study the pattern before proceeding. You may change and alter lines in whichever ways are most pleasing to the ear. You may stop at any effective point! Try composing as a class and then in small groups. Take your time. It's worth it!

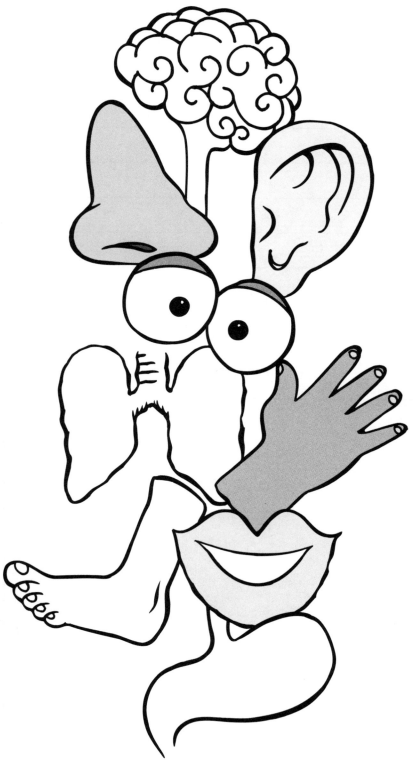

A Body Pantoum

1   Take care of your body—you won't get another
2   Yours is a complex working machine
3   Parts meshing in harmony
4   You are here with a lifetime guarantee

5-2   Yours is a complex working machine
6   In partners with brain and soul
7-4   You are here with a lifetime guarantee
8   Its wonders--a cosmic mystery

9-6   In partners with brain and soul
10   Respect the miracle of your life
11-8   Its wonders--a cosmic mystery
12   The rhythm of life beats sight unseen

13-10   Respect the miracle of your life
14   Take pride in your body with a sense that's keen
15-12   The rhythm of life beats sight unseen
16   Never abuse it--never misuse it

17-1   Take care of your body—you won't get another!

Greta B. Lipson

You Are a Fine Creation

Student Page

Name: _____

> ### *The Belly and Its Members*

My thoughts about this story: _____

_____

_____

_____

_____

_____

_____

Draw a picture from this story.

Believe in Yourself
Beowulf

Believe in Yourself
Beowulf

It was very long ago, in the year 655 that King Hrothgar built a great stone castle for his army of brave soldiers in Denmark. He called it Herot Hall. It was an amazing building. It was stronger than any human weapon of war.

One would think that finishing this new castle was a reason to celebrate–but all was not well. There was a frightening problem in the land that the king was not able to solve. For 12 years the king and his followers were tormented by a monster. His name was Grendel. He was more frightening than any enemy the king and his soldiers had ever faced.

Grendel was neither man nor beast but looked like a huge giant, covered with tangles of matted fur! He lived in scary

swamp with slippery lizards, giant rats and man-eating creatures. Even they were afraid of him. He lived deep in the marsh and came out to hunt for prey. Some said that there was another monster, even more terrifying, who lived in that nasty place with him. That awful creature was Grendel's mother--sometimes called a she-wolf!

Not many could escape Grendel when he was looking for food, but some who had seen him said that he walked upright and shook the land with the weight of his powerful body. He looked around, staring out of dark red eyes deeply set in a huge head. His chest was enormous and as he tore through the countryside he slobbered and growled.

He ate everything within his reach--grinding and tearing his way. Every living thing fled from his path.

On one warm summer night, the king and his brave soldiers were in Herot Hall prepared to set aside all problems and celebrate the glory of the new castle. They were a hearty group of comrades, relaxing and eating a magnificent supper, telling stories–laughing and entertaining one another. As strange as it may seem, their happy human sounds of enjoyment traveled to the swamp where Grendel heard them. Human happiness made him furious, and he gathered up his anger and set out for Herot Hall under cover of night. Little did the king and his soldiers know that the dreaded monster would soon bring an end to their party.

Grendel followed the sounds of laughter to the hall. By the time he arrived, everyone had fallen into a deep and satisfying sleep from so much good food and revelry. The strong fortress shook under the weight of the monster as he tore off doors and stomped from room to room. It was a hideous sight–walls crushed, furnishings and draperies ripped to shreds. Grendel killed 30 of the king's strongest soldiers.

The news of this nightmare traveled far and fast to the neighboring country of Sweden, and it was there that the hero of this piece heard the terrible story. His name was Beowulf, Prince of the Geat Tribe. He vowed that he would help the king and his people. Beowulf took 14 of his bravest soldiers, and they sailed to Denmark where he was determined to put an end to the monster.

Beowulf was a great hero, famous for his great strength and goodness. But he did not look like a hero! Those who met him could not believe that this mild-mannered person was capable of such remarkable achievements! His childhood was not easy, for he was deserted by his father and was brought up in the home of his maternal grandfather. At first he was lazy and undisciplined but then, as he grew under loving care, he learned and changed.

Beowulf did not boast. He did not strut. He was not handsome. As in fact, he was really quite ordinary-looking.

One would never take much notice of him around other men. Beowulf's name meant "the bee hunter," and in truth he had grown up with serious physical problems. It was reported that as a child he had been attacked by a swarm of bees and had to be kept in a dark room for many months to heal. The stings had left him almost blind, but as in everything else, he did not bear a grudge. Beowulf simply went on in life to do the best he could.

This strange-looking little man had great strength inside. People were attracted to him. He was an inspiration to ordinary folks who wanted to face everyday problems with courage. By his example, he showed them the way. He would only say, "Try your best and prove to yourself that you are capable. Work hard to be good at something, and it will give you confidence!"

When Beowulf and his men arrived at Herot Hall, there was a grand celebration and a feeling that finally someone had come who could rescue them from the monster. They all slept sweetly that night. None of them knew there was more horror on the way. For Grendel came to visit once again as if he had heard the news of Beowulf's arrival. The nightmare unfolded.

They were all asleep, except Beowulf who was the only warrior not caught by surprise. The stench of Grendel filled the hall and energized Beowulf to seize the monster. He crawled up Grendel's back like a nipping flea on a dog's hide, teasing and pounding with fists of iron. He was careful not to face Grendel but tormented him from behind. Beowulf was fast and sure with his sword, piercing and jabbing into the same wounds over and over again. Grendel screamed with rage at the man on his back whom he could not shake loose–and who caused him such pain.

Finally, Beowulf, in one superhuman effort, grabbed the thrashing arm of the monster. He held it in a savage grip—twisting and turning, almost faint with the effort until—he pulled the arm out of Grendel's body. The bleeding beast, blind with agony, staggered out of Herot Hall struggling to return to his swamp to die. Beowulf hung the awful arm from the rafters of the hall to show his victory to the king's warriors!

Beowulf, the hero, was a realist. He knew he had one more battle to fight, for surely Grendel's mother would finally come out of the swamp to avenge her son. The soldiers cheered and asked for a word from Beowulf who could only say, "We are striving to do what is right. I cannot promise anything except that I will follow the light and try my best to succeed." Beowulf and the soldiers cautiously trudged to the swamp, aware of the danger that lay in wait. At the edge of the swamp Beowulf took in a great breath and stepped into the murky deep, alone.

Immediately he knew he was in grave danger as Grendel's mother embraced her enemy silently and pulled him deeper and deeper into her lair. Beowulf told himself over and over again that he was fighting for all that was right, and he must rid the land of these horrible monsters.

Out of self-confidence and a determination to protect a peaceful community, Beowulf won the struggle with Grendel's terrifying mother. Some said he won because he carried an enchanted sword. Others swore he was saved by magic. Most knew that he conquered this evil force because of his spiritual strength and his willingness to try his best.

See *Cliff Notes on Beowulf*, Cliff Notes, Inc., by Elaine S. Skill, Ph.D., Lincoln, NE 68501.

Beowulf: A New Telling, by Robert Nye, © 1968, Farrar, Straus, Giroux, NY.

Beowulf, Retold by Rosemary Sutcliff, © 1961, Dutton, NY.

Believe in Yourself
Student Activities

- Most of us have had the experience of being so afraid of failure that we won't even rise to the challenge! Write a little note to yourself that begins with the sentence: "I didn't want to try because . . ." What were you afraid would happen? Now, write another note to yourself that starts: "I did try . . ." (And what happened?) What made it please you? Just how did you feel? The incident may not have been a success but was important to you at the time because you surprised yourself.

- Take the following question home so that you can interview friends, family or schoolmates: "If you try to do something and you fail, what do you think will happen?" Bring your answers back to class and discuss the answers you received. Promise the people you interviewed that you will not use their names. What words of advice would you give to others?

- The most inspiring stories about the will to succeed come from people who are disabled, physically challenged or handicapped in a variety of ways and have gone on to great levels of achievement! Organize a class project to highlight these amazing men and women by assigning groups to research musicians, artists, athletes, scientists and others. Following are examples of people and their accomplishments:

Evelyn Glennie is a percussionist from Scotland. She plays 50 instruments and performs with the world's great symphony orchestras. She has been profoundly deaf since she was 12 years old but has always been devoted to music. She can be observed removing her shoes for a performance so that she can "hear" the music through the soles of her feet!

Jim Abbott was the pitcher who won a gold medal in baseball in the 1988 Olympics. He was named his country's top amateur athlete, was a quarterback for the University of Michigan and was a professional pitcher for the California Angels. He was born without a right hand and learned to play baseball starting at age 6!

68

Chris Burke was born in 1965 in New York City and from the time he was nine years old, he wanted to be an actor like the people he saw on television. He told everyone he wanted to be an actor and one day he went to an audition for a part in the television series called *Life Goes On*. He earned the part and was on the program for several years. The astonishing thing is that Chris has Down's syndrome which affects people with mild to serious mental retardation.

Stephen Hawking was born in 1942. While studying at Oxford and Cambridge in England, he learned that he had Lou Gehrig's disease. He is one of the world's great minds and a brilliant theoretical physicist. In 1988 he published a nontechnical explanation of his work entitled, *A Brief History of Time*. He has been paralyzed by his disease, is confined to a wheelchair and cannot speak or move. He talks through the mechanics of a voice synthesizer and continues to teach and work.

Henry Ford (1863-1947) was the inventor of the gas-powered automobile and mass produced the Model T car which changed the face of American transportation. He said: "Whether you believe you can or believe you can't, you are absolutely right!" In a class discussion, examine Ford's meaning. (Teacher: think self-fulfilling prophesy.) Take a pro or con position on this statement and be tough in defense of your position!

- Organize into small groups for the purpose of writing a front page, recounting the courage (and handicaps) of that unlikely, but determined guy, Beowulf, who vanquished Grendel! Examine the front page of your daily paper for clues, and then write as if you were on the scene!

- In this story the monster Grendel is a very important character. The teacher may review the description of this frightening creature for careful listening. Work with a partner. A supermarket bag will be your main item. Try to make the scariest mask of Grendel anyone has ever seen. You may use paints, markers and crayons. You may also use objects to paste on the mask. Work slowly and carefully. Be prepared to show your mask to the class with your partner. One of you may wear it while the other explains some of the things you have done to make it unusual!

Believe in Yourself

Name: _____

> *Beowulf*

My thoughts about this story: _____

_____

_____

_____

_____

_____

_____

Draw a picture from this story.

Care About Something Outside of Yourself
With All My Heart

Care About Something Outside of Yourself

With All My Heart*

The statue in the city square had been standing looking over the city for a very long time, but there was not much known about its history. Probably the birds enjoyed it most of all, gathering on its shoulders and nestling near the cheek. The statue was called The Happy Prince, which some thought was a little foolish.

He was decorated in gold, which no one believed to be real, of course. It was rumored that the large red stone in his sword was a genuine ruby and that his eyes were real blue sapphires. But nobody believed that either! Who could be so wasteful as to use real jewels on a statue? It was unthinkable.

The fall winds blew in–swirling dry leaves in the square and with the change in weather the small, graceful swallows began to leave for the south country for warmth and comfort over the winter. There was, strangely, one swallow who had waited a little too long. He seemed

reluctant to leave the excitement of the city square to join his friends. "One more night," he thought, "and then I will fly away and join my companions."

He settled down, nestling on the collar of the statue protected, he thought, by the statue's big ears. "Well, at least I have a golden bedroom for the night," and he tucked his head under his wing and prepared to go to sleep.

"What's this?" he said, disturbed by a drop of water on his head. "There are no clouds, there is no rain--I'll move to the top button of the statue's vest--right under his big chin! It should be dry there." But once again he was annoyed by an even larger drop of water. "I don't have to stay here and be miserable," he thought. As he prepared to leave for a better shelter, a great pouring of water forced him to look up at the statue.

*Adapted from "The Happy Prince," by Oscar Wilde, 1888.

He couldn't believe what he saw--there were tears in the eyes of the statue! "I don't understand this! What's going on? Who are you? Why are you crying?" He craned his neck and looked up as hard as he could.

A low deep voice came from the statue who said, "When I was alive my life was protected. I played all day, had good things to eat, beautiful clothes to wear and friends who were as rich as I! My mother and father made sure that I knew nothing of other people who lived hardworking ordinary lives. What is more, I didn't really care about anyone but myself."

The little swallow found this very disturbing and didn't know what to say.

"After I died they built this statue and called it The Happy Prince. They should have called me The Foolish Prince--The Selfish Prince--The Know-Nothing Prince, for living such an empty life. Even though I had a human heart, it was untouched by the sorrow of other people."

The swallow listened politely and began to understand why this golden statue should weep.

The statue continued, "Now that I stand so high above the city I can see clearly all its ugliness and poverty. There are so many decent working people who don't have enough money to keep body and soul together." At that moment he looked far off and said, "Right now, in the distance I can see a miserable old house where a mother and her son live. The mother looks tired, and she is working hard sewing fine stitches and seed pearls on a gown of white satin. It is a garment to be worn for the next party in the royal ballroom. Her fingers are raw from moving the needle in and out of the heavy fabric. Her little boy seems ill with fever as he lay bundled up on his bed. He is asking for some juice to soothe his sore throat, but his mother has nothing to give him."

The little swallow grew silent with concern. What could he do? What could anybody do, for that matter? He was only a bird. As if in answer to his question, the statue said, "Little swallow, do me this favor. Pick the ruby out of my sword and take it to that needy mother."

The little bird replied, "My friends are waiting for me in the south country. They will worry that something terrible has happened to me. I am not sure that I am able to help you!"

"Please," said the statue. "My feet are fastened to this pedestal forever and I cannot move. Do this thing for me and stay just another night."

The swallow could not refuse the statue. With a heavy heart he picked the ruby out of the sword and flew with it in his beak toward the sick child's house. While he was in the sky he observed more than ever before and understood more. He flew over the church with its guardian stone angels. He passed over a balcony where a lovely, rich young girl was talking. He overheard her speak of the gown she would wear to the dance. "I have ordered pearls and lace work to be sewn on my dress. I certainly hope it will be ready. You know how lazy dressmakers can be!" she pouted.

Finally, the swallow came to the house of the dressmaker and the sick boy. The mother had fallen asleep, exhausted, with her head on the table. The bird left the great ruby near her thimble so she would see it the moment she awoke. The little boy tossed and turned on his bed as the swallow flew gently overhead and fanned his head until the youngster fell quietly into a restful sleep.

When the bird flew back to the statue, he noticed that he felt quite warm even though the cold had become more severe. "You feel that way, little bird, because you are filled with the warmth of having done a good deed for someone!"

The following day the swallow announced once again to the statue that he must leave for a warmer climate before it was too late. But the prince pleaded with the bird to stay just one more night. "I see across the city a fine young writer who is living in an attic without proper heat or food. He can barely move his fingers to write, but he has a talent and a message that should be shared with all people. He will come to nothing without some help. We cannot leave him. Please be my messenger once again. Take out one of my rare sapphire eyes and drop it so that he will find it and have money enough to get him through these difficult times."

But the swallow began to weep. "I cannot pluck out your sapphire eye. It is too cruel. Please do not ask me to do this."

But the statue commanded the bird to do his bidding and the swallow obeyed. He carried the precious gem to the unsuspecting writer who found it on his work table. The writer laughed and cried with joy. "At last," he said. "Someone who admires me has given me this costly gem to sell. The money will support me and help me pay for my food and rent. It will make my efforts so much easier until I finish my manuscript. I have been blessed."

The swallow knew now that he must leave or be destroyed by the cold. "I am coming to bid you good-bye," he said to his beloved statue. "If I stay longer, the frost will be upon us and I will not be able to fly to the south country at all."

As you may have guessed, the statue had another task for his messenger to perform. He wanted to help a poor little hungry girl selling penny matches on the street. The statue had nothing left but one sapphire eye. When he implored the swallow to pick out his last jeweled eye and take it to the child, the swallow cried, "Please don't do this. You are asking me to make you blind. I cannot bear any more of this!" As before, when the statue begged him, the sorrowful bird plucked out the sapphire eye and took it to the unfortunate child.

It is hard to believe that the statue would ask for still one more favor, but he did. "I am covered with genuine gold," he said. "Strip every bit of the precious metal off me and deliver it to people who care for little children with loving grace. Be fast, my gentle messenger, and do well."

Having done this task, the bird returned to the prince and said, "You are blind now, dear statue, and stripped of all your glory. I will never, ever leave you again." That night a hard frost moved in without mercy. The temperature dropped to chill the blood, and the swallow sat on the shoulder of his beloved statue, hugging close, speaking of friendship and timeless joys. They talked of the soaking warmth of summer--of bright blue skies--of sun-dipped afternoons and fragrant flowers.

By dawn the sun rose in the eastern sky and the little bird lay dead, at the feet of his beloved statue. The prince no longer looked regal but rather quite shabby and dull. "What's this?" asked the Mayor. "I've never noticed how ugly this mass of metal looks! The city square is no place for this eyesore! Take it down immediately," he commanded.

He rubbed his hands and gloated. Secretly the mayor yearned for a statue of himself to be put in its place.

They melted the statue in the local foundry where a workman raking through the materials noticed something very strange. He found a lead heart, almost broken in two among the rubble. Why, he wondered, didn't it melt in the furnace? He shrugged his shoulders and threw it on the dust heap where there was the cold still body of a small dead swallow.

Some people believe that the gentle bird is now in paradise. It is there that he sings sweetly at the left hand of the prince who praises human goodness and compassion.

Care About Something Outside of Yourself
Student Activities

- The prince looked back on his life as being selfish and not concerned with others. When he became a statue looking over the city, his vision of the world was enlarged and he changed. What conditions do you believe can help people change for the better? Are there situations that help people change for the worse?

- John Donne (1573-1631) was a poet who believed that we are all part of the world and humankind. He wrote in his sonnets, "No person is an island, entire of itself . . ." Think about your community and everyone and everything in it that contributes to your development as a well-rounded person: schools, museums, libraries, concert halls, theaters, churches, businesses, banks, hospitals, courts, etc. Organize a project to produce a class mural which represents all these community influences on your life. Draw, paint, color, cut and paste as you all improvise along the way. Write a small legend explaining the meaning of the mural.

- The prince was concerned about others and his role before and after he became a statue. He developed a quality called "insight" (the ability to see the true nature of things). Look this up in the dictionary for discussion. Draw an imaginative picture involving your inner eye and the act of looking into yourself with understanding.

- The swallow did not fly to the south country as soon as he should have, but he found a "safe haven" with the statue who grew to care about the bird. We all need a safe haven in our lives and it can be a person, a place or a thing that gives us comfort and protection. From what you know or understand, what is a safe haven for some people? What is your safe haven? (grandparents, a friend, a teacher, your aunt, your dog, your own room, the backyard, a park, etc.)

- In the story, "Care About Something Outside of Yourself," there was a great deal of giving and receiving. What are some of the ways in which you or your class could do something for the community in the spirit of giving? Think about helping senior citizens, working with primary school kids or physically challenged students, protecting the environment, enhancing your school on Arbor Day or organizing a used book sale for raising funds. Brainstorm ideas in class for community service which can actually be implemented successfully and will give participants a rich, bountiful feeling!

- The prince wants to do things for other people to make his life worthwhile. In the same way, each of you can make a contribution. No matter how small it may seem to you, all small efforts add up to a large effort! Consider projects you can do as an individual or a group for your home, classroom, school or neighborhood. Give suggestions while the teacher writes them on the chalkboard. Think of something you can all do really soon: Clean up your playground, plant a tree, prepare a program of song for a nursing home, collect cans of food before a holiday, start a toy drive and bring in a toy which can still be used by a needy child, collect books which can be sent to children where there are no school libraries, organize a coat and sweater drive for all sizes to give to the Salvation Army or similar agencies that do good works.

TLC10080

Care About Something Outside of Yourself

Student Page   **Name:** _____

> *With All My Heart*

My thoughts about this story: _____

_____

_____

_____

_____

_____

_____

_____

Draw a picture from this story.

What Really Counts Is What's Inside You
TGTBT* Building

* TGTBT = Too Good To Be True

TLC10080

What Really Counts Is What's Inside You
TGTBT Building

> What really counts is what you are and what you can become on the inside–not what you are on the outside.
> –Anonymous

Fenton was an okay guy. He was smart in some ways and dumb in others, like most of us. He hung out with good old friends who had known him since grade school. His girlfriend, Leah Lightner, was younger, but she was way smarter than he and he knew it. They could easily talk about millions of things and he learned a lot from her. So everything was pretty cool at school and at home.

He was never accepted by the popular kids, but he did watch them--the good-looking kids with the great hair and the perfect faces who were the ones everybody envied. Once one of them called him "Dumbo" because of his outsize ears. Another time he heard "shnozzola" which he thought referred to his big nose. He tried to rise above it, but frequently, in his innermost heart, he wished he could be better looking and a member of that golden circle.

One day, on his way out of the supermarket, Fenton looked at the community bulletin board where there was a small advertisement. It said, "We guarantee to change your looks. Reasonable rates. Apply in person at the TGTBT Building." He read it over again and thought this was a mighty strange place for such an ad. Besides that, there was no mention of plastic surgery.

The address was at the edge of town, not near any other commercial buildings. Certainly not a place where one would just drop in on the way to somewhere else. Now he remembered. It's that dome-like building that looks a little like a white concrete bubble. He didn't remember a sign outside.

At first, Fenton smiled when he read the ad. "Sure they can change your looks. Why don't they say how? Why don't they give a telephone number?" It sounded stupid to him, but he was a curious guy and this was really bugging him. He made a decision right then to check out the building. The weather was fine for walking; it was early in the day, and he didn't have anything more important to do. Why not?

It took him about 15 minutes to get there. He had remembered correctly. The building looked like a laboratory of some kind. It was right at the sign that said, "YOU ARE NOW LEAVING THE TOWNSHIP OF PLEASANT RIDGE." The place was nice and neat on the outside. The flowers and grass were manicured carefully. They almost looked fake.

He walked into the foyer which was illuminated by the kind of light he thought they used in operating rooms--it almost hurt his eyes.

There wasn't a sound. It was as quiet as a morgue. "Now cut that out," he scolded himself, "Don't be a wimp!" At first he didn't know what to do until he noticed a sign over a flattened red object that said, "Press here for receptionist." A woman in a white coat appeared. She was business-like and introduced herself as Ms. Arcadia. "Yes, it's true," she said. "We can change everything about you, and it will cost you very little."

"What's very little?" he asked, trying hard to sound smart.

"Each time you come we will expect a payment of two dollars--just to show your good faith," she said, busily preparing a form.

"How can you charge so little and still be in business?" Fenton strained to hear her quiet response.

Press here

for receptionist

"We are funded by the government," she replied vaguely. "This isn't a business for profit." Her voice trailed off as she organized the papers she gave him to sign.

"That sounds like a pretty good bargain to me." He still didn't get it but was too embarrassed to admit he was confused. Besides, he wanted people to like him, and he didn't want to seem troublesome. He pretended to read the forms she had given him and he signed in his best writing.

"Now, Fenton, tell us what you want changed." Ms. Arcadia looked into his eyes with a steady serious gaze. She was a no-nonsense person--no smiles, no other conversation.

He hesitated. "Well, I've got to know how you're gonna do this. What are you talking about? Are you gonna go at me with surgery--like an operation?"

"No, nothing like that. Let me assure you–it's a painless procedure. Just tell us what you want changed about yourself physically, and we'll change it!" He thought her voice had an impatient edge.

Fenton smiled secretly and said to himself, "Oh sure. This is a fake–right?"

"Perhaps you'd like to start with your nose. It seems a little large for your face," said Ms. Arcadia.

He was impressed. He had looked in the mirror a zillion times and wished his nose was smaller! Somehow he felt no embarrassment. "Yeh, OK, I'd like a smaller nose!" She led him into another room with computers and unfamiliar gadgets. She helped him onto a rolling chair and pushed his head gently into a hooded machine. He felt a little scared inside the hood but didn't say anything. After all, nobody poked him with a needle or gave him anything to swallow. Why should a piece of hardware scare him?

"Put your chin on the rest. Lean forward with your forehead against the brace and look at the circle of little lights in the middle of the cone." His head was totally swallowed up in the hood of the contraption. "It is important that you don't move. If you need anything, press this button." She pushed it into his hand.

The lights were turned down low. He heard the steady hum of a computer as Ms. Arcadia sat at a monitor and worked. Fenton began to lose all sense of time. Did he fall asleep? He wasn't sure. Time passed. Ms. Arcadia stood up, turned on the bright overhead lights and said, "You will see the change on your face gradually. People will not notice your new nose immediately. Before you leave, make another appointment."

"You mean you're not finished?" he asked Ms. Arcadia.

"We know from experience that you will want more changes, especially when you see good results."

Indeed, in the following months he returned over and over again. He didn't know how

it was done, and he didn't really care. He had his ears and nose made smaller. His teeth were straightened and his chin reshaped. And best of all, he was sure they made him taller and improved his rotten posture!

He was an overnight success. The cool guys all seemed to want to hang out with him now, and the pretty girls were definitely interested. He saw less of Leah these days. Sadly he was often very bored with the dumb conversation of some of these kids (when they weren't looking in the mirror). He missed Leah's smarts and his old nerdy friends who had been his loyal buddies. He kept telling himself that these new friends were really great, but he felt that they didn't know or care about the real Fenton inside. Besides that--they didn't really have a sense of humor, unless they were laughing at someone.

After some deep thought he decided he would return to the TGTBT Building. He wanted to talk to someone and felt very lonely these days. Today he would do more than change his face. He wanted to talk to somebody because in a strange way, he wasn't quite pleased with his life.

84

On this day he went to the building without an appointment. As usual he went into the front lobby but could hardly squeeze past the door. There were large packing boxes stacked in the entryway. They were neatly placed, like everything else, and were labeled for shipment. Ms. Arcadia came into the lobby in her usual cool fashion. "You were not scheduled for today," she said."

"What's going on?" Fenton asked.

"We are moving today!"

"Moving? You've never said a word about moving!" He was shocked and his voice shrill. "You can't move!"

"And why can't we move?" she shot back.

"Because you didn't fill your part of the bargain," he blurted.

"I beg your pardon. We changed everything you asked us to."

His face was red with anger, "But I'm not any happier now," he said.

"You are badly mistaken, Fenton." Her voice was low and controlled. "None of the contracts you signed said anything about happiness. We agreed to change you physically. We filled our part of the bargain. We did not guarantee happiness. That's your business. It is certainly not in our power." She turned away from him as if he no longer existed. He knew the conversation was ended.

As she began to check off the items on her clipboard, he walked toward the door in a slump. He felt alone and friendless. Outside he saw an unmarked truck and a uniformed driver pulling away from the building. He walked a distance and turned back only once. Fenton could have sworn the TGTBT Building looked as if it were getting smaller, like a deflating, wrinkled balloon.

What Really Counts Is What's Inside You
Student Activities

• If you had the same supernatural opportunity as Fenton did to alter yourself in one way, what would you change? Do you think that physical change would make a difference in your life? Would it guarantee your happiness? Why or why not?

• We are not able to change ourselves in supernatural ways, as Fenton did, but it is possible to do things for ourselves through hard work, education and attitude. How would you like to change yourself in ways that are possible? What attributes or skills would you want to develop that you think would make a difference in your future?

• Because Fenton was not pleased with the changes he experienced, some people thought he was an ungrateful fool! Others would say that he was unhappy with his new "popular" life because he began to understand that there were other "internal" factors, more important than good looks! What do you believe? Was he a fool or had he become wiser? Divide into two teams to debate this issue.

• Chart out a time line for yourself with illustrations. Look into the future, 5-10-15-20 years from now. What do you hope to be doing at all those future stages of your adult life?

• There is a great deal written about celebrities, who may be famous doctors, lawyers, actors, scientists, writers, artists, inventors, business people, musicians, teachers, athletes or others. You cannot be someone else--but you can be like someone you admire! From all of these people, whom would you choose as a role model? Explain.

• If people had a window in their chests that revealed innermost thoughts and feelings, what do you think others would see? What would be revealed? Would everyone have to be more honest and genuine? Why?

• Fenton, the schoolboy, found a mystery building where he could put his head into a machine, and it would change any features of his face which he didn't like. He came out looking different each time he made a visit. Imagine how unusual he looked each time. Make two or more finger puppets each with a different nose, different eyes, ears, mouth or eyebrows. The teacher will hand each pupil a piece of paper 3" (8 cm) square. Draw Fenton's funny face in the middle with crayons. Then roll the paper into a cylinder shape so that it will fit over the size of your finger. Glue it shut, let it dry and fit it over your finger. Make each finger puppet bold and funny!

What Really Counts Is What's Inside You

Student Page

Name: _____

> ## TGTBT Building

My thoughts about this story: _____

_____

_____

_____

_____

_____

_____

Draw a picture from this story.

TLC10080

You Are Finer Than You Think
Redhead

You Are Finer Than You Think
Redhead

Ever since he could remember, he was called by nicknames which described his hair. He was called Red, Carrot Top, Rusty or whatever somebody dreamed up at the moment. Of course, it didn't help that his name was Robin. (That's right. And some folks called him Red Robin.) He always wondered why he couldn't have had the color of hair that most people had. How about a nice brown, black or blonde? He wouldn't care as long as it weren't so red!

His skin was creamy smooth and pale. He had to stay out of the sun and be careful that he didn't get sunburned. Besides that, of course, Robin also had freckles–too many to count on his cheeks and the bridge of his

nose. He wore a baseball cap most of the time–to hide his hair--and when he finally got a job at Burger Bust, he was thrilled to be wearing that silly little cap–the one with the picture of a little tubby guy who was bursting from eating so many delicious hamburgers.

But still Robin attracted attention with his curly, red hair sticking out from under his silly cap, but it was nothing more than usual. One day Mrs. Tomashiba came in with her four little kids. They were really nice kids, but Robin could see that they were fascinated by his hair. They would stand and look at him while waiting for their mother and giggle among themselves. He was sure it was about him. Finally they would take their trays to the table. At every opportunity they came back for a spoon, a napkin or anything, Robin thought, just so they could sneak another peek at his red hair and smile and whisper among themselves.

TLC10080

Once he decided to cut his hair really close to his head like a basketball player. He was sure that trick would make his hair less noticeable. But it didn't work. After a while Robin grew so uncomfortable with the attention of the Tomashiba kids that he decided to say something to their mother. It wasn't his fault that he had red hair! He didn't like it anymore than they did—but there was nothing he could do about it! But it was Mrs. Tomashiba who said something to Robin.

"I must apologize for my children staring at you so much when we come in. But they keep saying that you have the most beautiful hair they have ever seen in their lives, and they can't stop talking about it."

Robin was shocked as he listened to Mrs. Tomashiba. She went on, "If you don't mind my saying so, I must agree with my kids. You must be very pleased that you were born with such terrific hair. Even your freckles are a perfect match. Be thankful you look so great! When your customers mention you, they always smile—it's because you're so special. You'll never be mistaken for anybody else—that's for sure!" As she turned away he was sure she said, "Everybody's jealous of that hair."

You Are Finer Than You Think
Student Activities

- Believe it or not–people do say nice things about other folks behind their backs. It can be a great surprise to learn that others see your strong points and outstanding characteristics though you don't have a clue. Sometimes people feel too uncomfortable to give a compliment face to face! How would you feel if you could hear just a small portion of those compliments? What would you like to have people say about you?

- Let the teacher be the clearinghouse for compliments. Once a week, perhaps on Friday, when everybody can use a lift, conduct a Compliment Day! Pass out index cards to each student. At the top of the card write the name of the person for whom you have a compliment. All cards must be signed though the names will not be revealed. Make your compliments smart and rewarding.

The teacher, using discretion, will process these "morale boosters" to make certain that every single student is included in this panoply of positive strokes. After going through a selection process, the teacher will read a few cards every Friday. Any variation on the theme is most welcome. The teacher, as final arbiter, must make certain that all students are acknowledged equally, though for some it may require solicitous help from the "management."

- Did you ever receive a compliment that was so terrific that it blew you away? One student would not say what his compliment was, but he did say that they had to make all the doorways in his house bigger so he could get his head through! Use your artistic imagination and draw that scene. On the bottom of the paper, write the nicest compliment you ever received (if you are courageous enough).

TLC10080

• Robin wore a cap when he worked at Burger Bust, and it pleased him because his red hair was partly hidden under that hat! You can make a similar hat out of newspaper, glue it to make it stay in place, decorate it and actually wear it yourself. You will need a double sheet of newspaper.

1. Fold the sheet in half and in half again.

2. Fold two corners of the lower left and lower right toward the middle.

3. You will then have two bottom edges. Fold each bottom edge up to make a brim.

4. You may want to glue in strands of red hair (yarn or paper) to look like Robin's head.

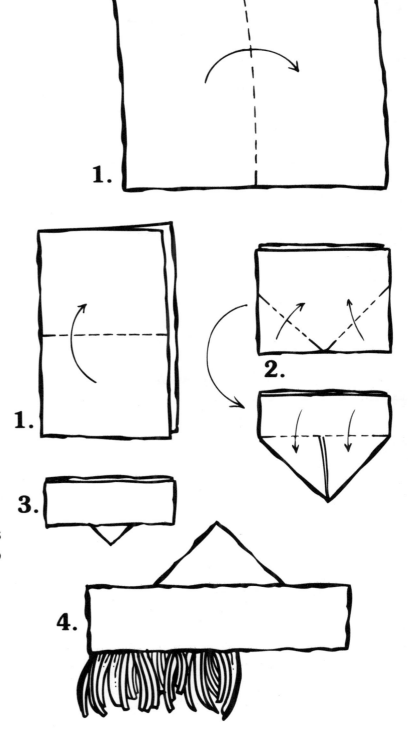

You Are Finer Than You Think

Student Page   **Name:** _____

Redhead

My thoughts about this story: _____

_____

_____

_____

_____

_____

_____

Draw a picture from this story.

TLC10080

I Am Important to Others
Don't Underestimate Yourself

- You don't have to be a superstar, a powerful athlete or a gigantic brain to be a most important person to others. There are many people who have ties to you because they love you as a relative, or because you are a friend, a classmate, a neighbor or an all-around good person. Think about it carefully and make a list of people who care about you and are connected to you. You may see yourself as being the center of a web with the following strands:

My name is Joe Zakaria.

I am:
> A son of Cleo and Ozzie
> A brother (or sister)
> Grandma Becky's tenth grandchild
> A safety patrol person
> A good baseball player on the team
> A student to my teacher
> A loving owner to my dog
> A good neighbor to Mrs. Franks
> A nephew to Uncle Oscar (and a helper)
> My Aunt Lilly's tallest nephew
> A good friend to Chuckie Schultz

- Now draw a tree (or actually make one with real branches, secured in a flowerpot or stationary base). Entitle it "My Family and Friends." Think of all your relatives, friends and contacts of all ages in the list above. Write those names on circles, squares or triangles which will be hanging from the branches. Decorate the tree with cut-outs of objects which interest you such as skates, balls, bats, books or stamps.

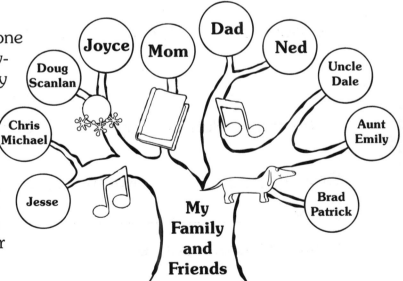

- A crest or a broad shield was a popular object in olden times which protected people and also identified the families to which they belonged. A shield could be large and covered with ornate patterns and pictures. Design your personal family crest or shield. Add items that point out the interests of your family such as sports, fishing, music, acting or scuba diving. One of our favorites is a shield that was designed with great things to eat with a knife and fork crossed over a plate.

A Day in the Sun

Special Award

Date: _____

_____
name

Has earned this certificate of honor for _____

_____

We congratulate our classmate on having won this special recognition!

Grade: _____   Room: _____

School: _____

City and State/Province: _____

_____

Teacher

_____

Principal

TLC10080